Spot the Differences

Rabbit or Hare?

by Jamie Rice

Bullfrog Books

Ideas for Parents and Teachers

Bullfrog Books let children practice reading informational text at the earliest reading levels. Repetition, familiar words, and photo labels support early readers.

Before Reading

- Discuss the cover photo. What does it tell them?

- Look at the picture glossary together. Read and discuss the words.

Read the Book

- "Walk" through the book and look at the photos. Let the child ask questions. Point out the photo labels.

- Read the book to the child, or have him or her read independently.

After Reading

- Prompt the child to think more. Ask: Did you know what rabbits and hares were before reading this book? Have you ever seen one?

This edition is co-published by agreement between Jump! and World Book, Inc.

Jump!
5357 Penn Avenue South
Minneapolis, MN 55419
www.jumplibrary.com

World Book, Inc.
180 North LaSalle Street, Suite 900
Chicago, IL 60601
www.worldbook.com

Library of Congress Cataloging-in-Publication Data

Names: Rice, Jamie, author.
Title: Rabbit or hare? / by Jamie Rice.
Description: Bullfrog books.
Minneapolis, MN: Jump!, Inc., [2022]
Series: Spot the differences
Includes index. | Audience: Ages 5–8
Identifiers: LCCN 2021028391 (print)
Jump! ISBN 9781636903491 (hardcover)
World Book ISBN 9780716646396 (hardcover)
Subjects: LCSH: Rabbits—Juvenile literature.
Hares—Juvenile literature.
Leporidae—Juvenile literature.
Classification: LCC QL737.L32 R53 2022 (print)
DDC 599.32—dc23
LC record available at https://lccn.loc.gov/2021028391

Editor: Jenna Gleisner
Designer: Michelle Sonnek

Photo Credits: Eric Isselee/Shutterstock, cover (top), 20; WildMedia/Alamy Images cover (bottom); patograf/Shutterstock, 21; Ana Gram/Shutterstock, 1 (left); JIANG HONGYAN/Shutterstock, 1 (right); godi photo/Shutterstock, 3, 8–9, 12–13, 23br; knelson20/Shutterstock, 4; WildlifeWorld/Shutterstock, 5; Erni/Shutterstock, 6–7 (top); Rachel Portwood/Shutterstock, 6–7 (bottom); FotoRequest/Shutterstock, 10–11; Pipedreams/Dreamstime, 14–15, 23tr; Agami Photo Agency/Shutterstock, 16–17, 23tl; Keith M Law/Alamy, 18–19, 23bl; Karin Jaehne/Shutterstock, 22 (left); allanw/Shutterstock, 22 (right); Serg64/Shutterstock, 24 (left); Colin Seddon/Shutterstock, 24 (right).

Printed in the United States of America at Corporate Graphics in North Mankato, Minnesota.

Table of Contents

How to Use This Book

In this book, you will see pictures of both rabbits and hares. Can you tell which one is in each picture?

Hint: You can find the answers if you flip the book upside down!

Long Ears

This is a rabbit.

This is a hare.

These animals
look alike.

But they are
not the same.

Can you spot
the differences?

ear

Both have long ears.
A hare's ears are longer.
They have dark tips.
Which is this?

Both have fur.

It gets lighter in winter.

A hare can turn all white!

Which is this?

Answer: hare

fur

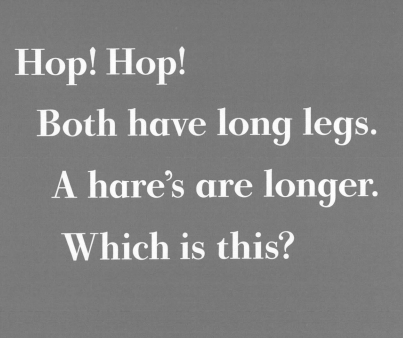

Hop! Hop!
Both have long legs.
A hare's are longer.
Which is this?

Both get chased.
Rabbits hide.
Hares run away.
Which is this?

Answer: rabbit

Rabbits dig burrows.
Hares make nests.
Which is this?

Baby rabbits are born with no fur.

Baby hares have fur.

Which are these?

Answer: hares

See and Compare

long
ears

fur

small
feet

long
hind legs

longer ears with dark tips

fur

big feet

longer hind legs

Quick Facts

Rabbits and hares are both mammals. This means they give birth to live young. They are similar, but they have differences. Take a look!

Rabbits

- live mostly in wooded areas, such as forests
- dig burrows under the ground
- hide when chased
- born without fur
- live in groups

Hares

- live mostly in open areas, such as prairies
- make nests above the ground
- run away when chased
- born with fur
- mostly live alone

Picture Glossary

burrows
Holes or tunnels in the ground that some animals use as homes.

hide
To go to a place where you cannot be seen.

nests
Places built by small animals to live in and care for their young.

tips
The end parts or points of things.

Index

To Learn More

Finding more information is as easy as 1, 2, 3.

❶ Go to www.factsurfer.com

❷ Enter "rabbitorhare?" into the search box.

❸ Choose your book to see a list of websites.